On th

Wild Warriors

Jim Pipe

A+
Smart Apple Media

Printed in the United States at Corporate Graphics in North Mankato, Minnesota.

Produced for Evans Publishing Ltd by White-Thomson Publishing Ltd
Edited and designed by Paul Manning

Picture credits
Front cover, Shutterstock/George Muresan; 3, 5, Shutterstock/Orla; 6, Dreamworks/Everett/Rex Features; 7, Shutterstock/Jose Ignacio Soto; 8a, Getty/Ted Spiegel; 8b, Corbis/Miguel Vidal 9b, Wikimedia Commons/Matthew Hunt; 10a, AFP/Getty Images; 10b, Wikimedia Commons/US Navy; 11, Wikimedia Commons/US Navy; 12, Corbis/Hamid Sardar; 13, Corbis/Marilyn Angel Wynn; 14, Wikimedia Commons/US Navy; 16, Photolibrary/Ken Welsh; 17a, courtesy Hammil Gallery; 17b, Shutterstock/Antonio Jorge Nunes; 18, Corbis/IDF; 19, National War Museum and Memorial Complex, Kiev; 20, Corbis/Yuiko Nakao; 21, Wikimedia Commons/Felice Beato; 22, Photolibrary/Fotosearch; 23, Oliver Thiele; 24a, Corbis/Yasukawa, Mitsu; 24b, Corbis/Gaz Faulkner; 25, Imperial War Museum; 26, Photolibrary/Karl Johaentges; 27, Corbis/Stringer Shanghai.

Every effort has been made to contact copyright-holders. If notified of any errors or omissions, the publishers will be glad to make corrections at reprint.

Library of Congress Cataloging-in-Publication Data
Pipe, Jim, 1966-
Wild warriors / Jim Pipe.
    p. cm. -- (On the edge)
Summary: "A wide-ranging survey of historical and current peoples involved in combat, from Vikings and Mongols to modern-day pirates, martial artists, and special ops. Includes quiz"--Provided by publisher.
Includes bibliographical references and index.
ISBN 978-1-59920-520-5 (library bound)
1. Soldiers--Juvenile literature. 2. Soldiers--History--Juvenile literature. 3. Military art and science--History--Juvenile literature. I. Title.
 U750.P57 2012
 355.3'309--dc22
                        2010054323

9 8 7 6 5 4 3 2 1

Contents

Fight to the Death

In ancient Rome, the skills of a warrior were highly prized—and few warriors were more skilled than the gladiators who fought to the death to entertain the crowds at the Roman games.

▼ Actor Russell Crowe clashes with an opponent in a duel scene from the 2001 Ridley Scott film Gladiator.

A gladiator's life in ancient Rome was brutal and mostly short. Some were trained to fight against wild animals. Others fought fierce hand-to-hand battles, often to the death. Enemy soldiers captured in battle were often forced to become gladiators, and spectators enjoyed watching these skilled fighters in action.

Audiences expected gladiators to die well—without begging for mercy. Many Romans died young, but they respected gladiators who met death with dignity.

An Epic Duel

At the first games to celebrate the opening of the Colosseum in Rome, two gladiators fought a memorable duel. In most contests, one gladiator was defeated and the emperor decided if he should live or die.

But Priscus and Verus fought so bravely and for so long that the crowd started shouting, "Free Priscus! Free Verus!" The fight went on until both men collapsed exhausted on the blood-soaked sand of the arena.

Finally, the Emperor Titus awarded victory to both men. He gave them wooden swords to show that they were now free men of Rome, and the two gladiators proudly walked from the arena through the "Gate of Life." The audience clapped and cheered as they left. The two men had faced death with courage, the sign of a true warrior.

▼ *Roman amphitheaters often contained trapdoors that allowed wild animals to be released into the arena. The Colosseum in Rome could even be flooded with water to simulate battles at sea.*

GLADIATOR SKILLS

Different gladiators had their own favorite weapons. Some carried oval shields and short swords, while others fought with small, round shields and curved daggers. Some gladiators used nets to trip their opponents and tridents (spears with three sharp points) to finish them off.

Raiders from the Sea

▶ *Viking longships were fast and nimble and could also be rowed up shallow rivers, deep into enemy territory. The word Viking means "raider from the sea."*

▼ *Warriors in horned helmets shout bloodcurdling battle cries during a modern reenactment of a Viking raid.*

Twelve hundred years ago, the Vikings were the most terrifying warriors on Earth. Using their dragon-headed longboats to sneak up on enemies, Viking raiders from Scandinavia attacked from the sea, combining surprise and terror to devastating effect.

For many days and nights, the Vikings pulled hard on their oars as their longboats battled the rough seas of northern Europe. After days at sea, the cry went up: "Land!" Whispering prayers to their gods, Odin and Thor, the Viking warriors strapped on their leather helmets and reached for their swords and axes.

As the ships reached the shore, the warriors leapt out into the shallow water, then tore up the hill toward the monastery. There was no escape for the terrified monks.

Going Berserk!

Some of the Viking warriors went into a battle frenzy. They howled madly, bit their shields, and slaughtered anyone who crossed their path. These "berserkers" fought with bare chests. In their rage, they believed nothing could hurt them. Within minutes, the ground was strewn with bodies, and flames were leaping from the monastery.

Holy Treasures

The Vikings killed sheep and cows and seized the holy treasures. Any monks who survived were taken away in chains to be sold as slaves. By the time the locals had gathered an army, the Vikings were long gone. Their chieftain was already thinking about the next raid and the booty that would surely be his.

▼ *Viking attacks on monastic communities such as Lindisfarne on the northeast coast of Britain spread terror throughout the Christian world.*

TODAY'S SEA RAIDERS

The Viking tactics of speed and surprise are still used today. In 2008, the Sea Tigers, members of the rebel group the Tamil Tigers, targeted a naval base in Sri Lanka. Using fast patrol boats, they attacked in the early hours of the morning. Within minutes, the navy camp was under their control.

A Plague of Pirates

Pirate raiders have plagued the high seas since ancient times, taking ships by force, looting cargo, and kidnapping crews. But if you thought pirates were a thing of the past, think again.

Looking at his radar screen, Captain Andrey Nozhkin feared the worst. A small speedboat full of heavily armed men was closing fast on his ship, the Danish-owned CEC *Future*. "We knew it was pirates, so we changed direction to make it harder for them to catch us," the captain said later.

◀ *Off the coast of northeast Africa, Somali pirates are a constant threat to ships and tankers. In 2008, one group seized 29 ships and earned $6 million in ransom money.*

Surrender or Die

The crew stood by to fight off the attackers with fire hoses. But when a rocket-propelled grenade whizzed past, the captain knew there was no choice but to surrender. After the pirates climbed on board, they ordered him to head to Eyl, a well-known base for Somali pirates.

The Ransom

The pirates demanded $7 million as a ransom for the crew. When the ship's owners tried to bargain with them, they threatened to capsize the ship. At one point, Captain Nozhkin and 12 others spent 24 hours cooped up on the tiny bridge of the ship. Tensions ran high.

After two months, a ransom was agreed. A plane flew over the ship. Once the pilot was sure the crew had not been harmed, he dropped a ransom of more than $1 million down to the ship by parachute.

Pitched Battle

When the pirates began dividing up the money, fighting broke out. "Some of them started shooting, while others fought with knives," said Captain Nozhkin. Soon one of the pirate leaders was dead, shot by his own men. Fortunately, none of the *Future*'s crew was harmed. After 68 days, the pirates finally handed back the ship.

⬧ *A U.S. Navy patrol boat closes in on a suspected pirate vessel in the Gulf of Aden off the coast of Somalia.*

BLACKBEARD THE PIRATE

One of the most feared pirates of all time was Edward Teach, alias "Blackbeard," who terrorized the Caribbean and east coast of North America in the early eighteenth century. In battle, Blackbeard carried pistols and cutlasses and wore lit matches in his beard to terrify his enemies. He was also said to cut the fingers off prisoners who were slow to hand over rings and valuables.

Horseback Warriors

For speed, power, and agility,
horseback warriors have always
had the edge over fighters on the
ground—and the thundering hooves
of a cavalry charge are a sure way
to strike terror into your enemies!

⏷ *Under their leader,
Genghis Khan, hordes of
Mongol horsemen swept across
Asia 800 years ago, amassing a
vast empire that stretched from
China to the Black Sea.*

In battle, Mongol horsemen often stunned their enemies with the speed and ferocity of their attacks. Here's how you can be like these fearsome warriors:

Lesson 1—Act Quickly
Rely on speed, not heavy armor. Mongol horses were small but quick and tough. They could scramble up rocks and race 62 miles (100 km) a day without tiring.

Lesson 2—Shooting and Riding
The Mongols were trained from youth to be expert riders and archers. They could shoot an arrow from horseback even when galloping at high speeds. It's going take you a few lessons to catch up. Beware—a long day in the saddle can make you very sore!

▼ A horseback warrior of the Shoshone-Bannock tribe in traditional dress

Lesson 3—Guard Duty
At night, your job is to guard the camp from wolves, enemies, and thieves. Mongol soldiers were known for their discipline and would willingly die for their leader, the great Khan.

Lesson 4—Tactics
You can learn a few clever battle tactics from Genghis Khan. When he faced a large enemy army, he pretended to run away. This led the enemy troops into a trap, as the wily old fox had already chosen where he wanted to fight.

Lesson 5—Fight Hard
Learning a few Mongolian wrestling tricks will give you some ideas when it comes to hand-to-hand combat. Show no mercy—and remember the Mongolian battle cry: "Ur Ah" (which gave us the word "hurrah").

NATIVE AMERICAN BRAVES
Like the Mongols, Native American tribesmen such as the Comanche and Sioux were highly skilled horsemen. A warrior's rank was shown by the markings on his horse and clothes and by the number of eagle feathers on his war bonnet. As well as bows and arrows, riders also fought with lances, clubs, and tomahawks.

Airborne Assault

The roar of the air rushing past fills the plane. The men clamber to their feet, struggling under the weight of their weapons and equipment. A red light flashes on and the paratroopers stream out the door. Four seconds later, they are floating to Earth. Four minutes later, they'll be fighting for their lives.

▶ A paratrooper gets ready for action over Dakar, Senegal, in East Africa. "Paras" can expect to be dropped into trouble spots anywhere in the world, often at short notice.

Airborne troops are trained to hit the enemy hard and fast, seizing airfields or bridges and destroying enemy weapons before the main forces arrive. They are among the best-trained soldiers in the world. They need to be.

Training for the Paras

Basic training for the UK Parachute Regiment, or "Red Devils," lasts about 28 weeks. In the early stages, recruits build up fitness on grueling speed marches and learn a range of outdoor and leadership skills.

Next comes a week of physically arduous tests. These include tackling an assault course 60 feet (18 m) above the ground and transporting huge weights in eight-man teams over 2 miles (3 km). Recruits also take part in a 60-second boxing match, which is not about winning or losing, but about showing how aggressive you can be. After a few more weeks of weapons training, parachute training begins.

Team Working

At the end of the course, only a third of recruits get to wear the famous maroon beret of the Parachute Regiment. To make the grade, you need supreme physical toughness. But paras aren't supermen: Just as important as strength and stamina are problem-solving skills and the ability to work in a team.

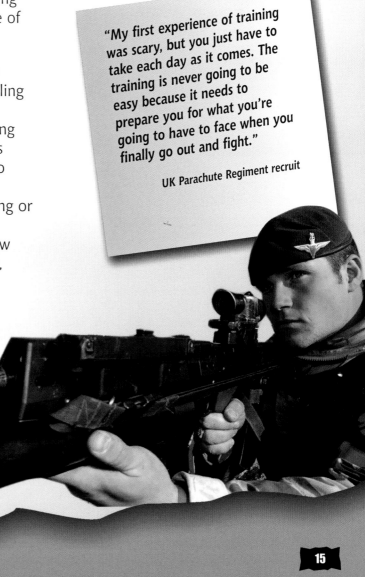

"My first experience of training was scary, but you just have to take each day as it comes. The training is never going to be easy because it needs to prepare you for what you're going to have to face when you finally go out and fight."

UK Parachute Regiment recruit

▶ *The modern Parachute Regiment provides support to Britain's airborne rapid deployment force. Paras also often work alongside "special forces" behind enemy lines.*

Born Warriors

Often standing over 6 feet (1.8 m) tall, Maasai warriors are an impressive sight with their beaded hair and red robes. In the past, they fought with lions and raided cattle from their neighbors. But in the 21st century, it's getting harder and harder for these proud warriors to keep their traditions alive.

In the West, people train to become soldiers as adults, but the Maasai people from East Africa are born warriors. Between the age of 14 and 30, young Maasai men live in isolation in the bush, learning tribal customs and developing strength, courage, and endurance—traits that have made the Maasai famous all over the world.

◀ *Armed with spears and shields, fierce Maasai warriors once carried out cattle raids throughout the Great Rift Valley of East Africa.*

Young Maasai boys are sent out with the calves as soon as they can walk. After a special ceremony at the age of 14, they spend up to eight years looking after livestock, often far from home. When the young men return to the village, they must undergo a painful initiation ceremony before they can become warriors and get married. Until recently, a young warrior also had to kill a lion with just a spear before being allowed to marry. Today, this is illegal, but lions are still hunted when they attack Maasai cattle.

Disease and Drought

In the past, the Maasai were feared throughout the region and often raided other tribes. But during the nineteenth century, the tribe was devastated by smallpox, droughts, and a disease that attacked their cattle. Over the last 150 years, many of the Maasai's traditional grazing lands have been turned into wildlife parks, ranches, or sites for new towns. As a result, many of the Masaai traditions are now in danger of dying out.

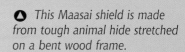

⬤ This Maasai shield is made from tough animal hide stretched on a bent wood frame.

⬤ One of the Maasai's most ancient traditions is the "jumping" dance, where young warriors leap into the air from a standing position to show their strength and agility.

Sisters in Arms

Do men make the best warriors? Not always. In modern armies, more and more women are fighting alongside male soldiers on the front line. And when it comes to flying a plane or driving a tank, skill, bravery, and a cool head are often more important than brute strength.

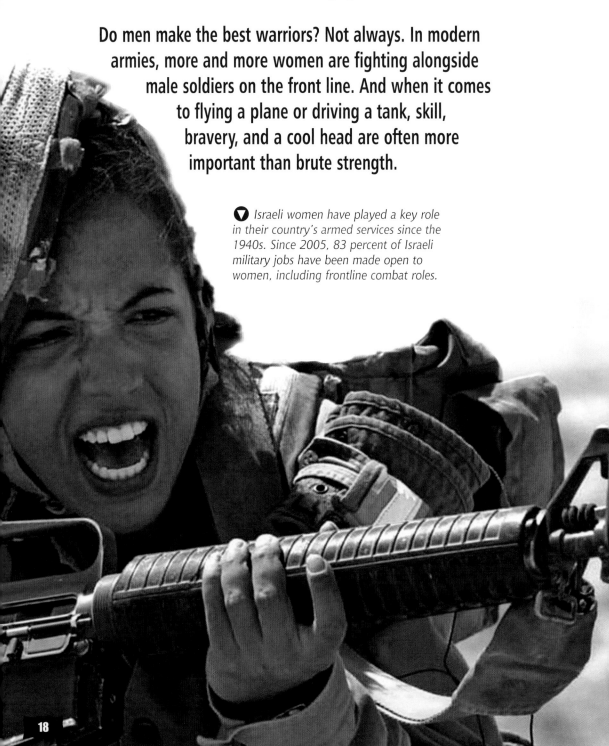

▼ Israeli women have played a key role in their country's armed services since the 1940s. Since 2005, 83 percent of Israeli military jobs have been made open to women, including frontline combat roles.

For most soldiers, it's tough enough just staying alive. But for women soldiers, there's the added challenge of earning the respect of their male comrades.

Revenge

When Mariya Oktyabrskaya (*right*) heard that her husband, a Russian army captain, had died fighting the Germans in August 1941, she was hungry for revenge. Selling all her possessions to buy a tank, she offered to donate it to the army on one condition—that she was allowed to be the driver!

The "Fighting Girlfriend"

Mariya's tank had "Fighting Girlfriend" painted on the turret in Russian. At first, many of her comrades viewed her as a joke. But not for long.

In Mariya's first battle, her tank was the first to break through enemy lines and destroy several pieces of enemy artillery. Over the next months, her reputation grew as a brave and able tank commander.

On January 17, 1944, one of the tracks of Mariya's tank was hit by a German shell. Disobeying orders, she climbed out and calmly repaired it on the spot, ignoring the enemy bullets whistling past her head. Just as she finished, Mariya was struck by shrapnel from a nearby bomb blast. She died in the hospital two months later. She was later made a "Hero of the Soviet Union," the Red Army's highest award for military bravery.

DEADLIER THAN THE MALE

When Roni Zuckerman became the first woman to train as a fighter pilot with the Israeli air force, she quickly proved that she could compete on equal terms with any man. Roni got her "wings" in 2001, after finishing sixth out of a class of 70. During dogfight training she even "shot down" her instructor!

The Warrior's Way

In medieval Japan, knights called samurai wore thick armor and helmets decorated with feathers, antlers, and even buffalo horns. Their chief weapon was a razor-sharp sword, the *katana*, which never left their side.

Samurai warriors followed a strict code of honor, called *bushido*, meaning "the way of the warrior." Reckless bravery and loyalty were highly prized, and a good samurai would fight to the death rather than surrender. "Bushido is like a mad death wish," said one sixteenth-century samurai. "It should take 50 men to kill you."

▲ In Japan, the skills practiced by samurai warriors gave rise to many other martial arts. Here, trainees practice kendo, a traditional form of fencing, with a two-handed wooden sword.

"Bushido is like a mad death wish—it should take 50 men to kill you."

Duel to the Death

With so much honor at stake, duels were common. Master swordsman Miyamoto Musashi (c.1584–1645) won his first duel at age 13 and went on to win 60 more without ever being beaten. It was said he rarely took a bath for fear of being caught without his sword and armor.

In a famous duel with his enemy, Sasaki Kojiro, Musashi was deliberately late. Some believe he waited until just before the tide changed so he could hop in his boat to escape Sasaki's men. Perhaps he was waiting for the sun to get in the right position so Sasaki would be blinded by it.

Either way, the duel was short. Musashi killed Sasaki using a wooden sword he had carved from an oar on the journey over to the island. Clearly the code of honor didn't rule out sneaky tactics!

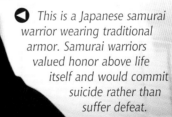

◀ This is a Japanese samurai warrior wearing traditional armor. Samurai warriors valued honor above life itself and would commit suicide rather than suffer defeat.

Dogfight!

Almost a hundred years ago,
pilots first fought each other in the sky.
To begin with, they threw grenades
and even bricks at each other from the
cockpit, but soon machine guns were
mounted on planes. The age of
the dogfight had begun.

 Flying a modern jet fighter is
like being on a rollercoaster. Tight
turns put an incredible strain on
your body, and "G-force" pressure
can make you black out or go blind
for a few seconds. You need to be
very fit to ensure your heart keeps
pumping oxygen to your brain while
you're spinning around in the air.

Things have come a long way since those early dogfights. A modern jet fighter flies incredibly fast—around 1,864 mph (3,000 km/h). Its jet engines can even point in different directions, allowing it to bank at high speed.

Thanks to onboard computers, pilots can focus more on their mission and less on the plane. A monitor inside the cockpit, called a "head-up display," allows them to read the instruments while keeping an eye on the sky. If there is an enemy plane nearby, the plane's sensors will spot it.

Aerial Combat

Flying a jet fighter is one thing; fighting in it is another. Modern fighters are armed with missiles that are fired long before the pilot sees the other plane. But planes can dodge these missiles—for example, by using flares to confuse a missile's heat-seeking device.

So despite all the new technology, dogfights do happen. One hundred years later, pilots still need nerves of steel and the ability to out-think their enemy. Perhaps things haven't changed so much after all.

▲ A replica of the triplane flown by the German fighter pilot Baron von Richthofen, alias the "Red Baron," during World War I

Soldiering by Stealth

From the days of Alexander the Great to World War II, secret operations have always been a vital part of warfare. Members of today's "special forces" operate unseen and unheard behind enemy lines. Their aim is to strike hard and fast—and without warning.

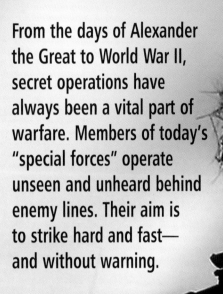

▼ *A British Royal Marine commando in full camouflage takes part in a training exercise in Scotland before being sent to fight in Afghanistan.*

◄ *Royal Marines from 42 Commando clear an area occupied by the Taliban during fighting in Helmand Province, southern Afghanistan.*

Special forces have stealth and surprise on their side, but they can often find themselves surrounded by much larger enemy forces. In 2001, one U.S. team was flown deep into the Afghan mountains by an MH-47 helicopter. Their mission was to work secretly alongside local forces to mount operations against the Taliban.

Horseback Journey

Special forces teams expect the unexpected, but the U.S. team was shocked when the Afghan leader, General Dostum, told them they would be traveling to his mountain headquarters on horseback. Their captain explained, "Six members of the team had never ridden a horse before. We were hundreds of meters up a cliff, and we knew if we fell, we'd be dead."

Mission Successful

Over the next few weeks, the team rode up to 19 miles (30 km) a day over some of the toughest terrain on earth. Sleeping in cattle sheds and mountain caves, the U.S. team lived and fought alongside some 300 Afghan soldiers.

In a few weeks, the squad destroyed several hundred vehicles and captured hundreds of enemy fighters, often using radios to call in air support. The operation showed how just a few skilled fighters could make a huge difference to the course of the war.

▼ Members of an SAS unit take part in an early desert mission in North Africa during World War II.

SSSH! IT'S THE SAS

The UK Special Air Services (SAS) was formed to carry out top-secret operations in Africa and Europe during World War II. In 1980, the normally publicity-shy SAS leapt into the headlines when live TV news showed SAS commandos storming the Iranian Embassy in London to free hostages held by Arab terrorists. The SAS has since become a model for special forces all over the world.

The Kung Fu Masters

In martial arts such as kung fu, experts use their hands, feet, and even their heads to defend themselves and overwhelm their opponent. Many of the moves, first developed thousands of years ago, are now being used by soldiers and military trainers around the world.

▼ Two monks demonstrate the art of kung fu at the Shaolin Monastery, Song Shan, Henan province, China.

According to legend, Chinese martial arts go back 4,000 years, when Chinese soldiers were first trained in hand-to-hand combat. Many different styles developed, and even peace-loving monks used the techniques to keep fit and control body and mind.

In the seventeenth century, the monks of the Shaolin Monastery in western China found themselves in conflict with the ruling Qin dynasty. They soon realized their graceful kung fu was far too slow to use for fighting. So five great kung fu masters came up with a new style of combat.

Eagle's Claw and Snake Fist

Hearing that the monks were plotting to bring down the Chinese royal family, the government sent an army to attack the monastery. The five masters fled and spread their style of fighting throughout China.

After escaping to the mountains, one of the five, a nun named Ng Mui, met a 15-year-old girl named Yim Wing Chun who needed her help. A local bandit was trying to force Wing Chun to marry him but had agreed to call the wedding off if she beat him in a fight.

Ng Mui created a new way of fighting that Wing Chun could learn quickly. It copied the movements of animals such as eagles, tigers, and snakes. Needless to say, the girl won the fight. To this day, the fighting style Wing Chun is named after her.

◀ A Shaolin monk breaks an iron sheet with his head during a performance at a temple in Quanzhou, Fujian province, China.

TAE KWON DO

In South Korea, army recruits learn tae kwon do ("the art of kicking and punching")—but not as you see it at the Olympics. When it's a matter of life and death, anything goes, so eye-gouging, breaking your opponent's knees, and "grab, twist, and remove" are all part of the game!

Wild Warrior Quiz

Are you tough enough to be a wild warrior? Try this easy-to-answer quiz.

1 Imagine you're a gladiator in ancient Rome. Your opponent is 6 feet (1.8 m) tall and built like a tank. Do you:

a Charge straight at him? Didn't someone once say that the bigger they are, the harder they fall?

b Wear him out by making him chase you, then get in close and look for gaps in his armor?

c Beg the emperor for mercy before things turn nasty? Facing death with honor isn't really your thing!

2 A Mongol warrior offers to show you how to fight from horseback. Do you say:

a "Saddles are for wimps. I'm riding bareback?"

b "How can I use a lance without getting knocked off myself?"

c "Isn't this a pedestrian zone? I'll walk, thanks."

3 Armed pirates are spotted closing in on your oil tanker. Do you:

a Tell the crew to repel invaders and fight to the last man?

b Radio for help and try to delay them coming on board? You don't want any wild shooting with all that oil around.

c Give the order to abandon ship—every man for himself!

4 As a samurai warrior, you follow a strict code of honor. If someone makes a joke about your lord and master, do you:

a Draw your sword and challenge the scoundrel to a duel with one hand tied behind your back to show you're not afraid to die?

b Demand a duel, but suggest another time and place so you have time to find out your opponent's strengths and weaknesses?

c Laugh and slap him on the back? Loyalty has its limits. You're not paid enough to die for your master.

Check Your Score

Mostly a Wow! You're a real Viking berserker—a danger to friend and foe alike!

Mostly b Like all the best soldiers, you're brave enough to take on the enemy and cool-headed enough to survive.

Mostly c When the going gets tough, you should get out of there. Who needs all that violence anyway?

Glossary

artillery large guns

bank to perform a turn in an aircraft

bridge the control room of a ship

bushido the code of honor followed by samurai warriors

camouflage disguise worn by soldiers to blend in with their surroundings

cavalry soldiers on horses

Colosseum a giant amphitheater in ancient Rome

commando a soldier specially trained to carry out raids

cutlass a type of curved sword

dogfight a battle in the air between fighter planes

drought when water becomes scarce and crops fail

flare a device that gives out colored smoke

frenzy a state of crazed excitement

gladiator a person trained to fight to entertain people

grenade a small bomb that can be thrown

initiation ceremony to celebrate a boy's coming of age

longship a wooden ship with oars and a single sail

monastery a religious community where monks live

oxygen gas contained in the air that is vital to life

para or **paratrooper** airborne soldier

pirate person who attacks a ship and steals its cargo

radar equipment for tracking ships and aircraft

ranch a type of large cattle farm

ransom money demanded by a kidnapper

rapid deployment force a military unit that can be moved quickly to wherever it is needed

shrapnel fragments of sharp metal

smallpox a type of infectious disease

stealth secrecy

surrender to give yourself up

tactic a plan to win a battle or fight

track part of a tank that allows it to travel over very rough ground

trident a three-pronged spear

turret part of a tank where the driver sits

war bonnet type of headdress worn by a native American

wings the uniform badge of a trained air force pilot

Web Sites and Further Reading

Web Sites

www.roman-colosseum.info/gladiators
Fascinating facts about gladiators in ancient times

www.pbs.org/wnet/warriorchallenge/vikings
Tour a Viking warship and find out more about these bloodthirsty warriors and their weapons.

www.nationalgeographic.com/pirates
Go on an animated adventure and learn all about famous pirates and their ships.

Further Reading

Gladiator (QEB Warriors), Deborah Murrell (QEB Publishing, 2009)

Knights (True Stories and Legends), Jim Pipe (Stargazer Books, 2010)

Pirates (True Stories and Legends), Jim Pipe (Stargazer Books, 2010)

The Vikings (Back to Basics), Loredana Agosta and Anne McRae (McRae Books, 2008)

Warriors: All the Truth, Tactics, and Triumphs of History's Greatest Fighters, James Harpur (Atheneum, 2007)

Index